BIBLE
FOOD
FUN

A STEP-BY-STEP COOKBOOK

LESLEY WRIGHT

LONDON • NEW YORK • SYDNEY • DELHI

www.dk.com

For Danni

Editor Jane Yorke
Art Editor Rachel Salter
Senior Managing Editor
Sarah Phillips
Deputy Art Director
Mark Richards
DTP Designer Megan Clayton
Production Linda Dare
Jacket Design Rachel Salter

Photography by James Jackson
Illustrations by Julie Downing

Published in Great Britain by
Dorling Kindersley Limited,
9 Henrietta Street,
London WC2E 8PS

2 4 6 8 10 9 7 5 3 1

Copyright © 2000 Dorling Kindersley
Limited, London

All rights reserved. No part of this publication may be reproduced, stored in a retrieval system, or transmitted in any form or by any means, electronic, mechanical, photocopying, recording, or otherwise, without the prior written permission of the copyright owner.

A CIP catalogue record for this book is available from the British Library.

ISBN: 0-7513-7261-7

Colour reproduction by
Colourscan, Singapore
Printed and bound in China by L Rex

DK would like to thank the following people for their help in the making of this book:
Paul Bailey for photography assistance,
Lauren Banyard and Karen Beckwith
for hand-modelling.

Cook's Safety Rules

Cooking is great fun, but it's important to read these safety rules before you start work in the kitchen.

1 Always wash your hands before preparing food. Protect your clothes with an apron, roll up your sleeves, and tie long hair back out of the way.

2 Read through your chosen recipe carefully. Gather together all the cooking utensils you will need. Prepare a clean work-top to work on.

3 Collect up all the listed ingredients. Weigh and measure your quantities following either the metric or imperial measurements.

4 Never start cooking without an adult being present. Whenever you see this oven glove safety symbol in a recipe, take extra care and ask an adult for help.

5 Always ask an adult to turn the oven on and off for you. Never handle hot pans, baking trays, or liquids without adult help. Wear oven gloves whenever you need to pick up hot, or even warm, things.

6 When cooking on the hob, keep pan handles turned to the side so that you cannot knock them over.

7 When stirring hot food in a pan on the hob, always hold the pan handle firmly as you work.

8 Be very careful when using sharp knives. Keep the knife blade pointing downwards and away from you and use a chopping board. Always prepare meat on a separate board not used for other foods.

9 Make sure that your hands are dry when plugging in and using electric appliances.

10 Use a cloth to wipe up any spills as you go along. Wash up your utensils once you have finished cooking and clean up any mess.

CONTENTS

4 BIG FISH PIZZA

7 DANIEL'S CHEESY LIONS

10 DOUBLE-DECKER FISH FEAST

12 EASTER BREAD CROSSES

15 EVE'S APPLE CRUMBLE

18 NOAH'S ANIMALS

21 ANGEL CAKES

24 JOSEPH'S SUNDAE BEST

26 CHOCOLATE MOSES BASKETS

28 SQUASHED FLY BISCUITS

30 BETHLEHEM STAR BISCUITS

3

God sent a great big fish through the stormy sea to swallow Jonah.

BIG FISH PIZZA

You will need

Baking tray • Rolling pin • Sharp knife
Tin opener • Mixing bowl • Fork
Butter knife • Chopping board
Cheese grater • Pastry brush

Y ou can make a scrumptious pizza by following this quick and easy recipe. Turn over the page to see the finished fishy dish.

Ingredients for 1 large pizza

295 g (10 oz) pack pizza base mix – made up according to pack instructions

2 tablespoons tomato purée

400 g (14 oz) tin chopped tomatoes

1 teaspoon mixed herbs

1 tablespoon cooking oil

115 g (4 oz) cheddar cheese

Salt and pepper for seasoning

Flour for dusting the work-top

Toppings

115 g (4 oz) chopped ham

1 courgette

225 g (8 oz) tin sweetcorn

4 cherry tomatoes

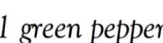
1 green pepper

1 black olive for decoration

Jonah and the big fish
Jonah was a person who learnt a hard lesson. When God asked him to do something, Jonah thought it would be too difficult and ran away to sea. He was thrown overboard during a big storm. Then a wonderful thing happened. God sent a huge fish to rescue Jonah. Find out how this fishy tale ends by reading Jonah 1–2.

Making the pizza

1. Set the oven to 220°C/ 425°F/ Gas Mark 7. Dust the worktop with flour. Roll out the pizza base dough into a large oval shape.

2. Use a butter knife to cut out a large fish shape, as shown. Place the pizza base on an oiled baking tray and put to one side.

3. Open the tins of sweetcorn and tomatoes and drain well. Mix the tomatoes in a bowl with the herbs and salt and pepper.

4. Next wash the courgette, tomatoes, and green pepper. Use a sharp knife to chop them up into thin slices for the fish scales.

5. Use a butter knife to spread the tomato purée all over the pizza base. Cover with the mixture of chopped tomato and herbs.

6. Grate the cheddar cheese and sprinkle it all over the pizza base. Put an extra layer of cheese on the fish's head and tail.

Decorating the pizza

1 Decorate your big fish pizza with the sweetcorn, chopped ham, and sliced toppings in curved rows to look like fish scales.

2 Brush the scales lightly with oil and place your big fish pizza in the oven. Bake for about 30–35 minutes or follow pack instructions.

Did you know?
The fish was an early Christian symbol. Many Christians still use it today.

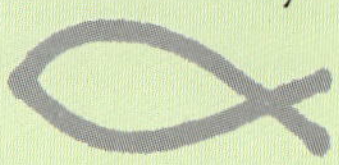

Look and see if you can spot the symbol when you're out and about.

Fishy meal
Decorate your big fish pizza with all your favourite tasty toppings.

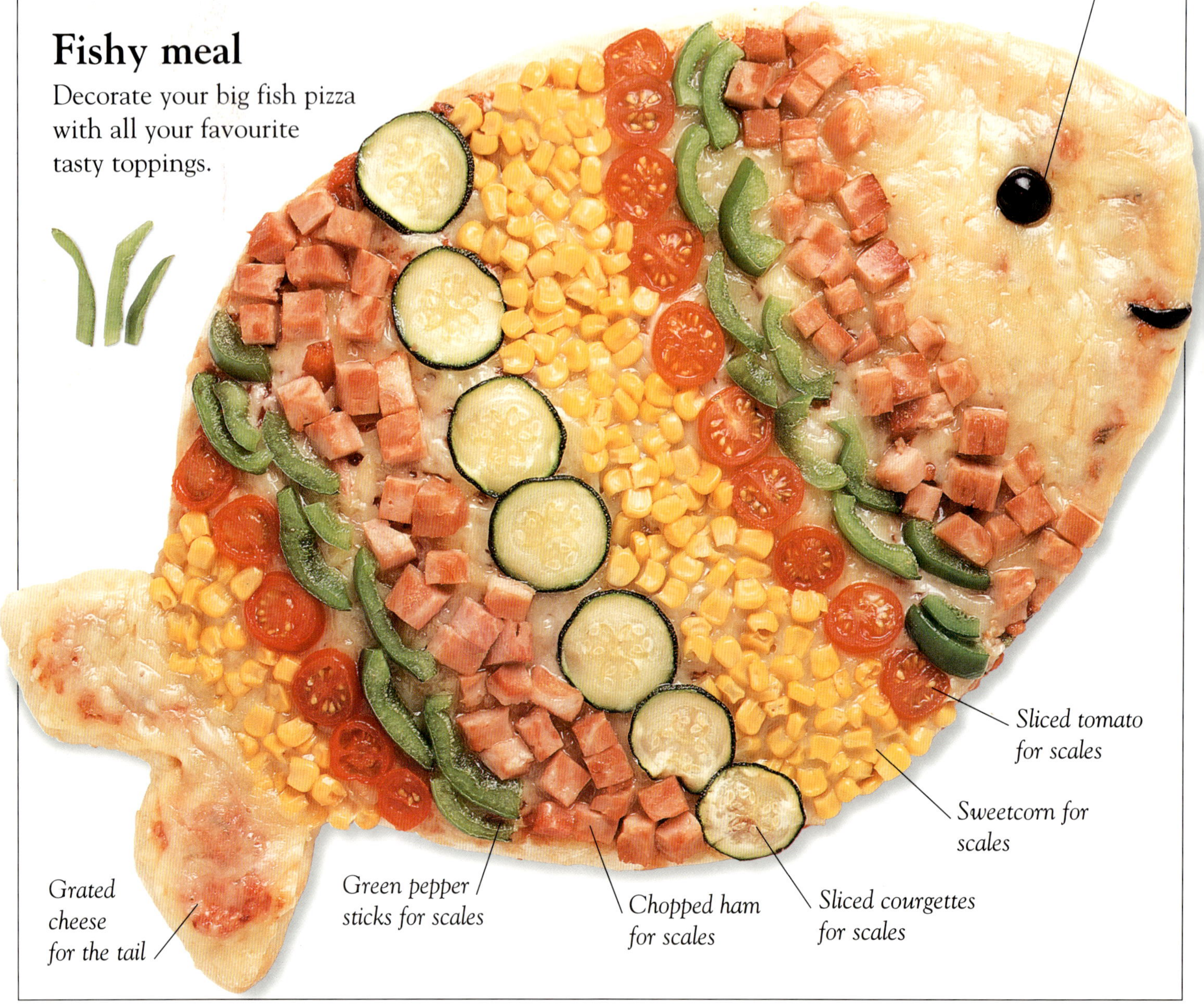

Olive slices for the eye and mouth

Sliced tomato for scales

Sweetcorn for scales

Sliced courgettes for scales

Chopped ham for scales

Green pepper sticks for scales

Grated cheese for the tail

6

King Darius gave orders for Daniel to be thrown into the den of lions.

Daniel's Cheesy Lions

If you're roaring hungry, try baking these cheesy lion scones. Follow the steps below and over the page and make a teatime feast that will satisfy every appetite.

Daniel in the lions' den
Daniel was a good man who trusted in God. He continued to pray even after King Darius passed a law to stop people from worshipping God.

You will need

6 cm (2½ in) round cutter
Baking tray • Mixing bowl
Sieve • Rolling pin • Scissors
Cheese grater • Pastry brush
Sharp knife

Ingredients for 4 lion scones

225 g (8 oz) self-raising flour

1 teaspoon baking powder

Pinch of salt

½ teaspoon mustard powder

 45 g (1½ oz) butter

115 g (4 oz) cheddar cheese

 150 ml (¼ pint) milk

4 black olives for decoration

Making the lions

1 Set the oven to 220°C/ 425°F/ Gas Mark 7. Sift the flour into a bowl. Add the baking power, mustard powder, and salt.

2 Grease and flour a baking tray. Rub the butter into the flour with your fingertips until it looks like breadcrumbs.

Making the lions continued

3 Grate the cheese and mix into the bowl. Add enough milk to bind the mixture together and knead it into a ball of dough.

4 Next dust your work-top with some flour. Roll out the scone dough until it's about 1 cm (½ in) thick all over.

Cheese scone face and mane

Sliced olive circles for the eyes

Snack attack

Serve your cheesy lions warm from the oven. Use sliced olives to make the lions' faces. Split the scones open and spread with butter to eat them at their best.

Olive pieces for the nose and mouth

5 Cut out four circles for the lions' faces and put them far apart on the baking tray. Knead together the rest of the dough.

6 Roll out the dough. Cut it into four strips 20 cm (8 in) long and 2.5 cm (1 in) wide. Snip all along one edge of each strip.

7 Carefully wrap the manes around the lions' faces. Gently press the dough together and spread out the manes.

Did you know?
In Bible times, lions were a symbol of power and were thought to be king of the beasts. King Solomon had a golden throne that was guarded by 14 lion statues.

Daniel in the lions' den
Daniel was thrown into a den of hungry lions because he refused to bow down and worship false gods. Miraculously, Daniel was saved from harm because God sent an angel to take care of him. Read Daniel 6 to find out what happened to Daniel's enemies.

8 Use a pastry brush to glaze each lion with milk. Bake the scones in the oven for 10–15 minutes until golden brown.

Jesus used five loaves and two fish to feed a crowd of 5,000 hungry people.

DOUBLE-DECKER FISH FEAST

This yummy tuna club sandwich can be fixed in a flash and will fill you to the brim – who knows, there may even be some left over!

You will need

Tin opener • Sharp knife
Chopping board • Butter knife
Fork • Small mixing bowl

Ingredients for 1 round

 3 thick slices brown bread

115 g (4 oz) tin tuna fish

1 tablespoon mayonnaise

Cucumber

 Lettuce

1 tomato

1 tablespoon cream cheese

2 cocktail sticks

Did you know?

Most people ate fish in Bible times because meat was expensive. People didn't have fridges like we do today, so they kept fish from rotting by salting it and drying it in the sun.

Five thousand hungry people
Jesus had been teaching the crowds all day, and the people were hungry. The disciples found one small boy with a lunch of five loaves and two small fish – nowhere near enough food to feed over 5,000 people. Jesus blessed the meal, and an amazing thing happened. When the disciples handed out the food, everyone was able to eat with plenty to spare. How many baskets of food were left over? Read Mark 6:30–44 to find out if you guessed right.

Making the sandwich

1. Open the tin of tuna fish and drain it. Put the tuna in a bowl and use a fork to mix the fish with the mayonnaise.

2. Toast or grill the slices of bread and chop off the crusts. Shred some lettuce and cut the cucumber and tomato into slices.

3. Spread the bottom slice of toast with cream cheese. Add a layer of tomato and lettuce. Next add a second layer of toast.

4. Cover with a layer of tuna mayonnaise and cucumber. Top with the toast and hold it all together with cocktail sticks.

Super sandwich

Cut your double-decker sandwich in half and enjoy your mouth-watering meal. Remember to remove the cocktail sticks before you take a bite.

Toasted bread · *Cocktail stick* · *Sliced cucumber* · *Tuna mayonnaise layer* · *Cream cheese layer* · *Shredded lettuce* · *Sliced tomato*

God's only son Jesus died on a cross to save the whole world from their sins.

EASTER BREAD CROSSES

You will need

Mixing bowl • Sieve • Sharp knife
Measuring jug • 2 baking trays
Wooden spoon • Scissors
Pastry brush • Cling film

Ingredients for 4 bread crosses

340 g (12 oz) strong white flour

225 ml (8 fl oz) warm water

1 teaspoon salt

15 g (½ oz) butter

½ sachet (2 level teaspoons) dried yeast

2 tablespoons cooking oil

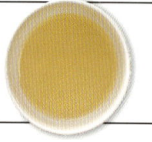
Poppy seeds for decoration

Celebrate Easter by baking some special bread rolls. Follow these simple steps and find out how to shape your dough into delicious bread crosses. Turn over the page to see the finished baked bread.

Making the dough

1. Set the oven to 230°C/ 450°F/ Gas Mark 8. Oil and flour two baking trays. Sieve the flour, salt, and yeast into a bowl. Rub in the butter.

2. Make a well in the mixture and stir in the warm water to make a soft dough. Add more flour if it's too sticky, more water if it's too dry.

The first Easter
Jesus was nailed to a wooden cross beside two thieves. Before he died, Jesus asked God to forgive the people who plotted to kill him. One soldier who heard this said, "Truly, this is the Son of God." Jesus' body was laid in a tomb and sealed with a huge stone. But what happened three days later? Find out by reading Matthew 28.

3. Place the dough on a floured work-top. Fold the dough from top to bottom and firmly push your knuckles into the centre.

4. Give the dough a quarter turn and knead it again as before. Repeat this process for about 5–10 minutes. Cut the dough into four.

5. Roll each piece of dough into a sausage shape 28 cm (11 in) long. From one end, cut off a short sausage measuring 10 cm (4 in).

6. Use scissors to snip a small wedge out of each sausage. Place the sausages together on a baking tray in the shape of a cross.

Baking the crosses

1. Brush the crosses with oil and sprinkle with poppy seeds. Cover with cling film and leave the dough to rise in a warm place.

2. After about 15 minutes, bake the crosses in the oven for 15 minutes. Test your baked bread. It should sound hollow when tapped.

Did you know?
The cross has been the main symbol of Christianity since the end of the 3rd century.

Some Christians wear a cross around their neck as a reminder that Jesus died to save us from our sins.

Poppy seed decoration

Cross-shaped bread roll

Easter bread rolls
These golden-brown bread crosses taste wonderful served warm with butter. Make them to enjoy with your family on Easter Sunday.

God told Adam and Eve they could eat the fruit from any tree, except one.

EVE'S APPLE CRUMBLE

This apple pudding has easy-to-follow steps and is deliciously tempting – treat yourself to a second helping!

You will need

22 cm (8½ in) round pie dish
Sharp knife • Potato peeler
Chopping board • Wooden spoon
Saucepan • Lemon squeezer
Cheese grater • Mixing bowl
Sieve • Large metal spoon

Ingredients

 675 g (1½ lb) cooking apples

1 tablespoon lemon curd

 1 orange

½ teaspoon cinnamon

 115 g (4 oz) plain flour

85 g (3 oz) butter

 55 g (2 oz) rolled oats

55 g (2 oz) demerara sugar

Butter for greasing

Adam and Eve
The first man and woman on earth were Adam and Eve. God gave them the beautiful Garden of Eden and told them to care for all the plants and animals that lived there. But God gave Adam and Eve one rule – he told them never to eat the fruit from one tree that grew in the garden.

Making the crumble

1 Set the oven to 190°C/ 375°F/ Gas Mark 5. Peel and core the apples, cut them into slices and place in the saucepan.

2 Grate the zest of an orange and put to one side. Squeeze the juice of the orange and pour into the saucepan with the apple.

15

Making the crumble continued

3 Add the lemon curd and cinnamon to the saucepan and cook gently on a low heat until the apples are soft.

4 Grease the pie dish with some butter. Spoon the apple mixture evenly into the pie dish and put to one side.

Did you know?
The forbidden fruit is not named in the Bible, but it is often illustrated as an apple. This is because the Bible was first translated into Latin, and the word evil was translated as *malum*, which also means apple.

5 Next, make the crumble topping. Sieve the flour into a mixing bowl and stir in the grated orange zest.

6 Add the butter to the bowl. Rub the butter into the flour with your fingertips until it looks like fine breadcrumbs.

7 Add the rolled oats and sugar to the bowl. Stir the crumble ingredients until they are well mixed together.

8 Sprinkle the crumble topping evenly over the apples and bake for about 30–35 minutes, until the topping is golden brown.

Apple delight

This hot fruit pudding is perfect for a cold winter's day. Serve your apple crumble straight from the oven topped with creamy custard or scoops of vanilla ice cream.

Adam and Eve
One day, Satan disguised himself as a talking snake and tempted Eve to eat the fruit from the forbidden tree. Eve shared the tasty fruit with Adam. Immediately, they both felt ashamed. What happened when God found out that Adam and Eve had disobeyed him? Read the rest of the story in Genesis 3.

Tangy apple-and-lemon filling

Crunchy crumble topping

Two by two, animals and birds of every kind went aboard Noah's ark.

NOAH'S ANIMALS

These mouth-watering sweets are very easy to make and need no cooking at all! Which is your favourite – the peppermint zebras or the lemon leopards?

You will need

Mixing bowl • Rolling pin • Whisk
Wooden spoon • Chopping board
Sieve • 2.5 cm (1 in) round cutter
Wire cooling rack • Parchment paper

Ingredients for up to 30 sweets

340 g (12 oz) icing sugar

1 egg white

2-3 drops peppermint essence

2-3 drops lemon essence

2-3 drops yellow food colouring

2-3 drops black food colouring

Noah's ark
God asked Noah, the one good man left in the world, to build a huge boat called an ark. He told Noah to fill the ark with a male and female pair of every kind of bird and animal. God wanted to save Noah, his family, and all the animals before he sent a flood to destroy the world. After the flood, which creature helped Noah to look for dry land? See how the story ends in Genesis 8.

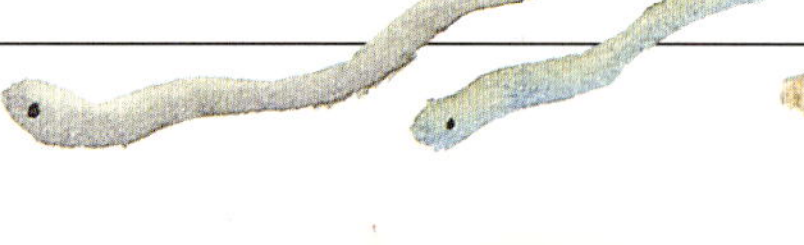

Peppermint zebra sweet

Lemon leopard sweet

Making the zebra sweets

1 Place a sheet of parchment paper on a wire cooling rack. Whisk up the egg white in a bowl until it's frothy, but not stiff.

2 Sift the icing sugar into the bowl a little at a time. Keep stirring the mixture with a wooden spoon until it goes stiff.

3 Work the mixture into a soft ball with your fingers. Divide the icing into three balls: two large and one small.

4 Knead the peppermint essence into a large ball of icing. Roll it out on a work-top dusted with icing sugar until it's 5 mm (1/4 in) thick.

5 Knead the black food colouring into the small ball of icing. Roll out strips and lay them on the white icing. Save the left-over black icing.

6 Roll out the stripy icing. Use the round cutter to cut out the zebra sweets and lay them on parchment paper to dry out.

19

Making the leopard sweets

1 Knead the lemon essence and yellow food colouring into the last ball of icing and roll it out. Add tiny balls of black icing.

2 Roll out the icing again and use the cutter to cut out the spotty leopard sweets. Leave the sweets on the parchment paper to dry.

Did you know?
Animals have different skin markings to camouflage them in the wild. A spotty coat helps the leopard to hide in the dappled light of the forest when it's hunting prey. A stripy coat helps the zebra to blend in with the rest of the herd and confuse attacking lions.

Spots and stripes

Arrange your sweets together on a plate to make a stripy zebra face and a spotty leopard face. Invite your friends to take their pick of these delicious sweet creams.

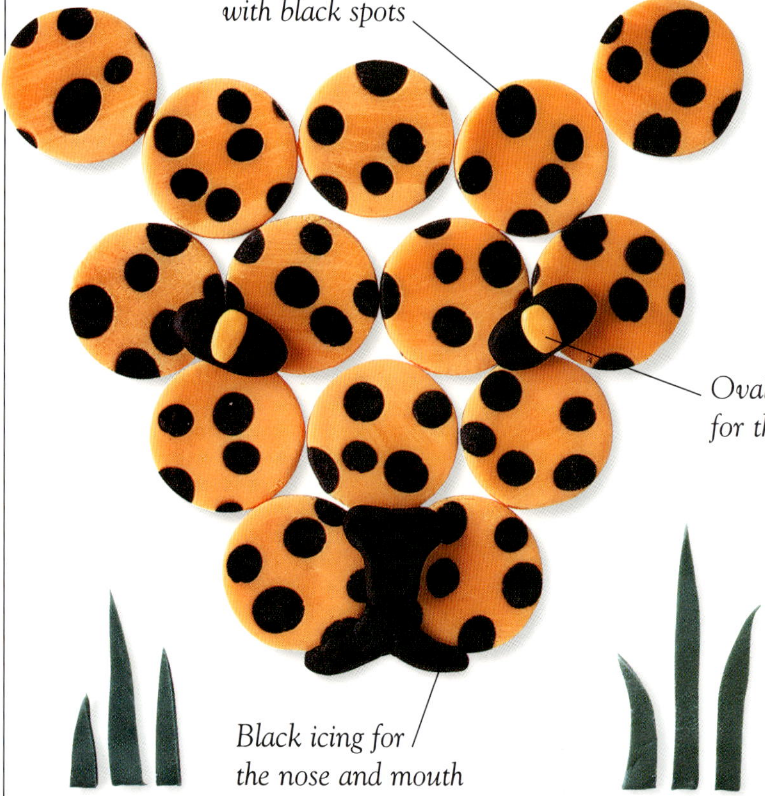

Peppermint cream with black stripes

Small ovals of black icing for the eyes

Lemon cream with black spots

Ovals of icing for the eyes

Black icing for the nose and mouth

An oval of black icing for the nose

20

The angel told Mary, "God has blessed you. You will give birth to a son."

ANGEL CAKES

These strawberry cup cakes are very quick to bake and they taste so divine, you would think they were made in heaven!

You will need

Mixing bowl • Small bowl
Wooden spoon • Tablespoon
2 bun tins • 2 teaspoons • Fork
Sharp knife • Chopping board
Wire cooling rack • Sieve
16 paper cake cases

Ingredients for 16 cakes

115 g (4 oz) self-raising flour

115 g (4 oz) caster sugar

115 g (4 oz) butter

2 eggs

1 teaspoon baking powder

2-3 drops vanilla essence

For the fillings

8 strawberries

150 ml (¼ pt) extra thick double cream

The birth of Jesus
God sent his messenger, the angel Gabriel, to tell a young woman called Mary that she was going to have a very special baby. Mary was engaged to be married to a carpenter called Joseph. The angel said that the baby was the Son of God, and that Mary and Joseph should name him Jesus.

Making the cakes

1 Set the oven to 200°C/ 400°F/ Gas Mark 6. Place the 16 paper cases into the bun trays. Wash the strawberries and cut them in half.

2 Cream the butter and sugar together in a bowl with a wooden spoon. Keep beating until the mixture is light and fluffy.

21

Making the cakes continued

3 Beat the eggs in a small bowl with a fork. Add the eggs a little at a time and beat into the mixture. Add the vanilla essence.

4 Sieve the baking powder and flour into the bowl, a little at a time. Gently fold the flour into the mixture with a large spoon.

5 Check that the cake mixture drops easily off the spoon. If it's too stiff, add a tablespoon of water and check the mixture again.

Did you know?
Angels are heavenly beings who carry God's messages between heaven and earth. Only two angels are named in the Bible. One is the angel Gabriel, who appeared to Mary. The other is the warrior archangel Michael, who fought against Satan.

The birth of Jesus
One night out in the fields, some shepherds were keeping watch over their flocks of sheep. Suddenly, a shining angel appeared in the sky and spoke to the frightened shepherds. The angel told them the wonderful news that a Saviour had been born in Bethlehem. When the shepherds went to worship the baby Jesus, where did they find him? Read about their visit in Luke 2:8–20.

6 Put a teaspoon of cake mixture into each paper case. Place the bun trays on the top shelf of the oven and bake for 15 minutes.

7 Let the cakes cool. Use a knife to cut a shallow circle out of the top of each cake. Cut the circles in half to make wings.

8 Fill the hollows in the cakes with cream and position the wings on either side of the cream. Decorate with half a strawberry.

Heavenly cakes

These delicious strawberry angel cakes just melt in the mouth. Enjoy them as a special teatime treat.

Cup cake

Thick cream filling

Juicy strawberry topping

Cake semi-circles for the wings

23

Jacob gave his favourite son Joseph a beautiful coat of many colours.

JOSEPH'S SUNDAE BEST

This colourful ice-cream treat is a fruity feast ready in minutes. Follow each simple step and let this delicious dessert brighten up your Sunday!

You will need

Sundae glass • Ice-cream scoop
Sharp knife • Chopping board
Sieve • Tin opener

Ingredients for 2 servings

 4 scoops vanilla ice cream

115 g (4 oz) strawberries

 115 g (4 oz) blueberries

2 kiwi fruits

 295 g (10 oz) tin mandarin slices

Making the sundae

1 Wash the fresh fruit. Peel and slice the kiwi fruit. Remove the stalks from the strawberries and cut into quarters.

2 Drain the tin of mandarin slices. Place a layer of blueberries in the bottom of each glass. Add a layer of mandarins.

3 Next, fill the sundae glass with a layer of sliced kiwi fruit, followed by a layer of chopped strawberries.

4 Add two scoops of vanilla ice cream. Finally, decorate with strawberries, blueberries, and a slice of kiwi fruit.

Rainbow fruits

Make up your own sundae recipes using seasonal fruits and your favourite ice-cream flavours.

Did you know?
In Bible times, people often used natural things to make different coloured dyes for clothes. Blue dye came from pomegranates, yellow dye from almonds, purple dye from shellfish, and red dye from insects.

Strawberries, blueberries, and a slice of kiwi fruit for decoration

Yellow layer of vanilla ice cream

Red layer of strawberries

Green layer of kiwi fruit

Orange layer of mandarin slices

Blue layer of blueberries

Joseph's colourful coat
Joseph's multi-coloured coat was a special gift from his father, but it made his 11 brothers very jealous. The brothers decided to get rid of Joseph, so they sold him as a slave to some merchants travelling to Egypt, where he ended up in jail. However, God gave Joseph a special skill. Look in Genesis 41 to find out what the skill was and how it helped to change Joseph's life.

The princess found a baby boy in a basket floating among the bulrushes.

Chocolate Moses Baskets

You will need

Saucepan • Small bowl • Fork
9 paper cake cases • Rolling pin
2 teaspoons • Bun tray • Sharp knife
Chopping board • Cocktail stick

Ingredients for 9 cakes

 3 large shredded wheat biscuits

175 g (6 oz) plain chocolate

 225 g (8 oz) white fondant icing

 2-3 drops each of green, yellow, red, and blue food colouring

Try your hand at these crunchy chocolate treats. The little Moses figures are easy to make and taste as good as they look!

Did you know?

Moses was discovered in a basket made of papyrus reeds. The ancient Egyptians also used papyrus to make the first kind of paper. They wrote with pictures called hieroglyphs on this paper using reed brushes dipped in paints.

Moses in the bulrushes
In Egypt, Pharaoh gave the order for all the Israelite baby boys to be killed. One mother thought of a clever way to save her baby. She wove a basket out of dried reeds, placed her baby in the basket and hid him amongst the bulrushes in the River Nile. When Pharaoh's daughter came down to the river to bathe, she discovered the baby and decided to adopt him as her son. Who do you think the princess paid to look after the baby for her? Find out in Exodus 2.

Making the baskets

1. Break the chocolate into a bowl. Place the bowl in a saucepan of water over a low heat. Stir until the chocolate melts.

2. Break the shredded wheat biscuits into small pieces. Add them to the chocolate and stir until the wheat is well covered.

3. Put the paper cases in the bun tray. Spoon some mixture into each case. Use the back of a spoon to press a hollow in each basket.

4. Cut the icing into four. Roll out two pieces and cut into 18 parts. Form nine simple baby shapes and nine circles for shawls.

5. Cut the remaining icing into four pieces. Knead different food colours into each one. Roll out the green icing. Add coloured stripes.

6. Use a rolling pin to flatten the stripy icing. Cut out nine blankets and place over the babies in the chocolate baskets.

Baby's eyes made with a cocktail stick

Stripes of red, blue, green, and yellow icing for the blanket

White icing shawl wrapped around baby Moses

Chocolate-covered shredded wheat for the basket

Chocolate treats

These pretty chocolate Moses baskets are perfect for serving at a party. Leave the baskets to harden in a cool place by storing them in an airtight container.

27

God said, "Let my people go, or I will send swarms of flies to cover Egypt."

SQUASHED FLY BISCUITS

You will need

Mixing bowl • Sharp knife • Sieve
20 cm (8 in) sandwich cake tin • Fork
Wire cooling rack • Wooden spoon

Ingredients for 8 biscuits

 85 g (3 oz) plain flour

85 g (3 oz) cornflour

 115 g (4 oz) butter

55 g (2 oz) caster sugar

 55 g (2 oz) currants

Caster sugar for sprinkling

These tasty shortbread biscuits are very easy to bake, just follow this simple recipe. Invite your friends to take a bite, but tell them to watch out for the flies!

The plagues of Egypt
God called Moses to lead his people out of Egypt. Moses asked Pharaoh many times to let God's people go, but Pharaoh wouldn't listen. So God sent ten terrible plagues to make Pharaoh change his mind. How many plagues can you name? Check your answers in Exodus 7–11.

Making the biscuits

1. Set the oven to 180°C/ 350°F/ Gas Mark 4. Cream the butter and sugar together with a wooden spoon until light and fluffy.

2. Sieve the flour and cornflour into the bowl. Add the currants and knead the mixture into a soft dough.

3. Grease and flour the cake tin. Press the dough firmly into the tin and prick all over with a fork. Bake for 40–45 minutes.

4. Once the biscuits are baked, mark the cutting lines with a knife and leave to cool. Finally, sprinkle the biscuits with sugar.

Did you know?
The seventh plague of Egypt was a storm of hailstones. The largest hailstones ever to have been recorded were the size of tenpin bowling balls. They fell in Kansas, USA and weighed an incredible 760 g (1 lb 11 oz) each!

Biscuit crunch
Cut up your squashed fly biscuits and place them on a cooling rack to harden. You can store the biscuits in an airtight container to keep them crisp and fresh.

Caster sugar topping

"Squashed fly" currants

Shortbread biscuit

The wise men saw a bright new star in the sky and followed it to Bethlehem.

BETHLEHEM STAR BISCUITS

You will need

Measuring jug • Wooden spoon
Sieve • Saucepan • Rolling pin
Parchment paper • 2 baking trays
Mixing bowl • Wire cooling rack
Large and small star cutters • Skewer
Chopping board • Pastry brush
Thin coloured ribbon

Ingredients for 20 biscuits

55 g (2 oz) butter

50 ml (2 fl oz) golden syrup

55 g (2 oz) sugar

115 g (4 oz) plain flour

½ teaspoon bicarbonate of soda

½ teaspoon cinnamon

½ teaspoon all-spice

10 fruit-flavoured boiled sweets

Confectioner's gold dust

Hang these spicy star biscuits on your Christmas tree and watch the light twinkle through their pretty "stained-glass" centres. Turn the page to find out how to display these festive, edible decorations.

Making the biscuits

1. Line the baking trays with parchment paper. Sieve the flour into a bowl. Add the sugar, spices, and bicarbonate of soda.

2. Set the oven to 180°C/ 350°F/ Gas Mark 4. Warm the syrup and butter together in a pan over a low heat. Stir until melted.

3. Pour the mixture into the bowl with the dry ingredients. Mix into a dough. Work the dough into a smooth ball with your hands.

The wise men
When the wise men in the East saw a new star appear in the night sky, they knew that a great king had been born. They followed the star all the way to Bethlehem. The wise men gave baby Jesus three wonderful gifts. Can you name them all? See if you are right by reading Matthew 2.

4 Dust the work-top with flour. Roll out the biscuit dough until it's 5 mm (1/4 in) thick. Use the large star cutter to cut out ten biscuits.

5 Place the stars on the baking trays. Use the small star cutter to cut out the centre of each biscuit. Put a boiled sweet in each hole.

6 Bake the biscuits for 10 minutes until golden brown. When the melted sweets have hardened, place the biscuits on a wire rack to cool.

31

Did you know?
Some scientists think that the large star the wise men followed may have been Halley's comet, which was first seen in ancient times. Others believe that the star was a supernova – a faint star that suddenly explodes and becomes brighter. Chinese astronomers recorded the appearance of such a star around the time of Jesus' birth.

Hanging the biscuits

1. Use a skewer to make a hole through one point of each star. Rub gold dust on to the small stars with your finger.

2. Carefully thread a length of thin ribbon through each hole and tie into loops. Hang up your stars as Christmas decorations.

Small golden star biscuit

Ribbon bow for decoration

Colourful boiled-sweet centre

Large spicy star biscuit

Twinkling stars
These colourful star biscuits will brighten up your Christmas tree and make perfect gifts for visitors. Keep your biscuits fresh in an airtight container until they are ready to put on the tree or eat.